LEADING CHANGE
in Your World

ACTION LEARNING GUIDE

This action learning guide to *Leading Change in Your World* may
be adapted for

- a ten-lesson on-line course format, with slight
  modification;
- a ten-part action learning tool to complement the
  text in courses;
- a ten-session guide in an intensive workshop
  or seminar.

Mark A. Smith
Larry M. Lindsay

Triangle Publishing
Marion, Indiana

 Triangle Publishing

Leading Change in Your World: Action Learning Guide
Mark A. Smith and Larry M. Lindsay

Direct correspondence and permission requests to one of the following:
E-mail: info@trianglepublishing.com
Web site: www.trianglepublishing.com
Mail: Triangle Publishing
                   4301 South Washington Street
                   Marion, Indiana 46953
                   USA

Scripture quotations are from the following sources:

Authorized King James Version (KJV), 1611.

Contemporary English Version (CEV), Copyright © American Bible Society, 1995. Used by permission.

The Living Bible (LB), Copyright © Tyndale House Publishers. Used by permission.

The Amplified New Testament (ANT), Copyright © The Lockman Foundation, 1954, 1958, 1987. Used by permission.

Smith, Mark A. and Lindsay, Larry M.
Leading Change in Your World: Action Learning Guide
ISBN 1-931283-11-7

Printed in the United States of America
Evangel Press, Nappanee, Indiana

TABLE OF CONTENTS

The Serenity Prayer

"God, give us grace to accept with serenity the things that cannot be changed, courage to change the things which should be changed, and the wisdom to know the difference."

Reinhold Niebuhr

Defining Change and Understanding Change Processes

WEEK 1

What is Change?

∽ OBJECTIVE ∽

The *Leading Change* learner will be able to define change, understand change processes, and see compelling needs to be an agent of change.

Assignments

1. Read Chapter 1 of the book *Leading Change in Your World*.

2. We encourage you to read the entire book during the first week. Then, go back and study each chapter, referencing the respective chapter with the lessons in this action learning guide.

Defining Change: Webster's New Collegiate Dictionary defines change as "to make an essential difference; to transform; to give a different position, course, or direction." Heraclitus wrote, "Nothing endures but change." If organizations intend to stay competitive and vibrant—in PRIME condition—the leaders must learn to lead change among people, teams, cultures, systems, structures, strategies, and programs. Constructive change then is synonymous with growth and improvement. Therefore, constructive change has to be expected, anticipated, planned for, and continuously experienced in today's fast-paced, globally competitive world. If corporations and businesses want to stay alive, they must learn to lead and facilitate change. Individuals and organizations that stay vibrant and current are the most responsive to change.

What Experts are Saying About Change: To focus our thinking so as to understand and accept the legitimate reasons for change (that is, to make things better), let's take a look at some pertinent quotes in the literature of change.

> "The frantic pace of change in a chaotic world tends to keep us spinning out of control, stressed and feeling as if we are being driven rather than driving" (Smith & Lindsay, xi.).

> "The more you change, the more you become an instrument of change in others" (Hendricks, in Smith & Lindsay, 1).

> "Change has considerable psychological impact on the human mind. To the *fearful*, it is *threatening* because it means that things may get worse. To the *hopeful*, it is *encouraging* because things may get better. To the *confident* it is *inspiring* because the challenge exists to make things better. Obviously, then, one's *character* and *frame of mind*

determine how readily he brings about change and how he reacts to change that is imposed on him" (Whitney, in Smith & Lindsay, 5).

"In a higher world it is otherwise, but here below to live is to change, and to be perfect is to have changed often" (Newman, in Smith & Lindsay, 25).

"The art of progress is to preserve order amid change and to preserve change amid order" (Whitehead, in Smith & Lindsay, 7).

Characteristics of Effective Change: Not all change is necessary or good. Change is ultimately either destructive or constructive. Of course, necessary change ought to be constructive. The purpose of change is to help us get better, improve, grow, renew, and refocus. What is the compelling need for change? Why should an individual, department, team, or organization change? Kotter explains five characteristics of effective or constructive change.

1. **Necessity** – In order to maintain a competitive edge, organizations and individuals must see that change is necessary.
2. **Urgency** – If change is to occur, a sense of urgency must propel the . . . company into action.
3. **Vision** – Vision molds and clarifies the need for change and assists in reculturing and structuring implementation.
4. **Communication** – Communication translates the vision and enables people to effect it.

5. **Teamwork** – Change is best realized when people's talents and strengths are coalesced (Kotter, in Smith & Lindsay, 6).

A Cause for Really Learning about Change Processes!

"In times of change the learners *inherit the world, while the* learned *find themselves equipped to deal with a world that no longer exists."*

Eric Hoffer

Leading in a Culture of Change—Seven Action Sets:[1] To be successful in today's fast-paced world, people and organizations— businesses, companies, schools, government, faith-based institutions— must be able to deal with the reality of accelerated cultural change. The most effective leaders today understand change processes and are able to lead in a culture of change. Following are seven action sets from leading authors of constructive change in organizations today (Adizes, Collins, Fullan, and Smith & Lindsay):

1. Right People in Right Places
2. Shared Vision That Inspires Optimum Results
3. Sense of Moral Purpose – Mission-Driven Organizations
4. Understanding Change Processes
5. Collaborative Relationships Among Employees
6. Team Learning: Creating and Sharing Knowledge
7. Engaging in "Making Sense Out of What We Do Best"

These action sets serve as a workable process for leading change in people and organizations. ***People improve and make more good things happen before organizations do.*** Engage in these seven action sets when facilitating change in people and units of the organization. We believe this will enable you to become effective at finding and implementing the best solutions for constructive change with the least amount of stress. They will help you and your team change continuously while remaining unified.

Leading Change Action Learning Lesson 1

Change is a process of feeling better, thinking better, and performing better in a relationship or situation that needs to be improved. In effect, it is a process of *making more good things happen and fewer bad things happen for yourself and others*. Change is a process of becoming the best you can be for the relationship, situation, and organization.

Task #1 for Lesson 1: Look at the "Organizational Culture Interview" outline following this section. First, we want you to reflect on these questions as they might pertain to you. Then, we encourage you to interview two to five or more people, preferably in a group setting, and ask these or similar pertinent questions.

Task 1.1 Interactive Action Learning
Organizational Culture Group Interview

1. Tell about a time recently when someone expressed appreciation to you.

   a. How did it make you feel?

   b. How does feeling appreciated or being complimented affect your work?

2. If you improve in your work, who notices and how?

3. How are employees made to feel special in this organization?

4. In what ways does the organizational culture bring out your best attitude and work performance?

5. People improve with practice and experience. In what ways are you more productive now than a year ago?

6. In what ways do you intend to be more productive one year from now?

7. What is your most perplexing problem?

8. How do you believe it can be solved?

9. What will this organization be like for you when it becomes even better?

10. Imagine it is one year later and this has been your best year ever. What happened to make it your best year ever?

"Can you imagine finding joy on the job every day?"

Task 1.2 Interactive Action Learning

What did you learn about yourself that surfaced as a compelling need for change—something that will make things better in your organization?

What did you learn about others in your sphere of influence that surfaced as a compelling need for constructive change—something that will make more good things happen and fewer bad things happen in their lives and within the organization?

Defining Change and Understanding Change Processes

WEEK *2*

Changing My World — Who, Me?

∽ OBJECTIVE ∽

The *Leading Change* learner will conduct a self-assessment and identify one personal area for constructive and necessary change (i.e., improve, make better, transform, head in a new direction).

Assignments

1. Read Chapters 1 and 2 of the book *Leading Change in Your World*.

2. We expect that you have read through the entire book during the first two weeks. Now go back, studying and referencing the respective chapters for Week 2.

A Model for Change: On page 8 of *Leading Change in Your World*, you will find the Smith & Lindsay Model for Change (Figure 1.2). Constructive change commences with seeing how to improve something in yourself, in others, or within a unit or organization. In the organizational culture self-assessment and interview you conducted with others in your sphere of influence, you discovered some things that needed to change. You also found some to be more intriguing or fascinating than others. This caused you to begin to move from current reality (what is) to a future vision. All change commences with an inspired idea or future vision (the best you can imagine) of how you can move from what is to what should be. That is the subjective or spiritual dimension of change. The process is one of *fascination-imagination-illumination-destination-determination-coordination-culmination.* This is the seeing/feeling/envisioning dimension of the change process for an individual, a relationship, or a unit. It is the emotional dimension—involving the passion and excitement of what it will be like to attain the desired change (Smith & Lindsay, 9-12).

Examining the Elements of Change: We first move through the seeing, feeling, envisioning dimension of a *Model for Change* in deciding to make a difference in our world. Here we identify the compelling need for change and the passion to lead change in this sphere of influence. Then we must follow an operational process—a set of individual action elements—that will move us from "deciding to change to implementing, monitoring and assessing the results" (pp. 8, 13-17).

Leading Change Action Learning Lesson 2

You conducted a type of self, or reflective, assessment in Lesson 1. Here you discovered some personal areas needing change, as well as the need to change something in people and systems within the unit or organization. Before embarking upon planned change, we encourage you to conduct one more self-assessment. Take a few minutes to study the Self-Assessment Chart (pp. 32-34).

Task 2.1 Interactive Action Learning

What were your most notable strengths?

How did this make you feel?

Task 2.2 Interactive Action Learning

Now list the areas you believe demonstrate an urgent and compelling need for you to change.

Given the list of areas you desire to change, assign point values for the list amounting to 100. For example, you may have listed four compelling needs. You assigned 40 points to one, 25 to another, 20 to another, and 15 to the fourth one. Which seems to be the most compelling or urgent? List it below. Begin to *see* it and *feel* it, so you can *change* it. I feel a compelling need to . . .

Task 2.3 Interactive Action Learning

SMART Goal: Write the compelling need as a *SMART* Goal (pp. 36-41). "This is something that I really want to work on over the next nine weeks and accomplish within the next quarter."

Task 2.3 Interactive Action Learning *(continued)*

Action Plan: Write five to seven action steps that you must take to achieve SMART Goal 1 (see p. 37).

Benefits: Visualize the attainment of the goal (See – Feel – Change). What benefits will achieving this goal bring you, others, and the unit or organization? Really "see" the attainment and list at least four or five benefits (see p. 38).

Defining Change and Understanding Change Processes

WEEK **3**

It Starts with a Decision: Deciding to Change!

✎ OBJECTIVE ✎

The *Leading Change* learner will identify one sphere of influence area that needs to be changed (i.e., heading in a new direction, improving, making better, transforming).

Assignments

1. Read Chapters 2 and 3 of the book *Leading Change in Your World*.

2. We expect that you have read through the entire book during the first two weeks. Now go back, studying and referencing the respective chapters for Week 3.

A Life-Changing Mission: Each of us has a responsibility to be a difference maker—to foster constructive change for people, units or organizations. We all have a sphere of influence. We all have a reason for being; however, in some cases, that purpose has not surfaced. What is your life-changing mission? What is your present reason for being? Perhaps you have a written mission statement. If so, meditate upon it, and see if there are ways to improve it. We find that our own mission statements change from year to year according to our life roles and cumulative knowledge, experience, and compelling needs. If you do not have a current mission statement, we encourage you to seize the opportunity to write one now (see pp. 44-48).

Write your current, revised, or new mission statement below. Try to write it in one clear, concise, and convincing sentence. See some examples on p. 45. Sample Mission Statement: *"To discover, model, relate, and teach empowering truths that enable individuals, teams, and organizations to experience optimal health, personal mastery, service to others, and leadership influence in the world."*

My mission is

What are four or five core values that might provide a strong foundation for your mission statement? Example core values might be: *health, humility, integrity, teamwork, being responsible, being productive, and so forth.* List the values that will cause you to stretch in *being the best you can be for others.*

My Core Values are

Leadership, Team Building, and Team Learning

WEEK 4

Forever Following, Forever Leading: Leadership Strategies

∾ OBJECTIVE ∾

The *Leading Change* learner will observe and reflect
upon key leadership principles and strategies
for twenty-first-century leaders.

Assignments

1. Read Chapters 3 and 4 of the book *Leading Change in Your World*.

2. We expect that you have read through the entire book during the first few weeks. Now go back, studying and referencing the respective chapters for Week 4.

Mega Leadership[2]

Much is being written today about transformational leadership, principle-centered leadership, adaptive leadership, theory Z leadership, servant leadership, good-to-great leadership, and team leadership. It is intriguing to study, observe, and listen to both the dialogue and the debate about the new emerging paradigm in leadership. Join us and take an in-depth look into five virtues for mega leaders.

Best Leadership Practices of Mega Leaders

In past years we have been hearing much about Jim Collins' research in *Good to Great* (2001). In this long-range study of good-to-great companies, Collins and his research associates noted two distinct leadership qualities of good-to-great leaders. Simply stated, they are "personal humility" and "professional will." The debate around the country seems to center on these two concepts. Of notable interest, people seem to be trying to develop a sense of shared meaning about what "personal humility" really means in corporate leadership, particularly unionized companies.

Collins writes of "good-to-great leaders" demonstrating personal humility and professional will. He defines a level-five leader as "an individual who blends extreme personal humility with intense professional will" (2001, p. 21). Maxwell writes of level five as Personhood/Respect (1993). He sees his understanding of level-five personhood as comparable to the level-five leaders that Collins describes. Recently, a group of leaders from across the country quoted Bob Buford as saying that level five is submission (Survival-Stability-Success-Significance-Submission). It is intriguing to see people wrestling with the issue of extreme personal humility as a virtue of great leaders, when so often it is the outgoing, charismatic, high-profiled hero leaders that we see and hear in the media. As we listen to leaders and emerging leaders discuss level-five or "mega" leadership, it is common to hear the following conclusions:

1. A level-five leader is a rare individual.

2. Level five is too soft for most of today's globally competitive, fast-paced organizations.

3. Humility, submission, personhood, and servant leadership virtues apply more to faith-based organizations than to the world of work.

4. Humility is a religious term and shows signs of weakness in competitive "tough love" work environments.

These conclusions, which we consider to be erroneous assumptions, have inspired us to look more deeply into the emerging leadership paradigm written by leadership authors such as Bennis, Collins, Covey, Greenleaf, Heifetz, Kouzes/Posner, Maxwell, Smith & Lindsay, and others. Great leaders are sorely needed in critical times such as ours.

Five Virtues of Mega Leaders

We have found that this debate was being waged by scholars such as Aristotle and Paul more than 2,000 years ago. It appears that the "spiritual dimension—the Judeo-Christian dimension"—makes the virtue of extreme personal humility so difficult to accept in the competitive and fast-paced workplace of today's Fortune 500 companies. Let's take a look at five virtues of mega leaders as presented by Paul (Ephesians 4:1-3 NIV).

1. *Humility*

2. *Meekness (Gentleness)*

3. *Patience*

4. *Love*

5. *Peace*

Collins	Maxwell	Lindsay
Level-five leaders are individuals who blend extreme personal humility with intense professional will. They are self-effacing individuals who display the fiercer resolve to do whatever needs to be done to make the company great. Collins, J. (2001). Good to Great. New York: Harper Business.	"Personhood/Respect: People follow because of who you are and what you represent. This step is reserved for leaders who have spent years growing people and organizations. Few make it. Those who do are bigger than life" (1993, 12).	Mega leaders reflect the virtues of humility, meekness, patience, love for others, and the bond of peace in what they think, say, and do in being the best they can for people and the organization (community) they are called to lead.

Focus on *Good to Great*. Humility is a word that was coined by early Christian believers. Basil described it as "the gem casket of all the virtues" (Barclay, 1958). Humility comes when we look deeply into ourselves and compare ourselves with "world-class" people. It is the ability to see honestly our weaknesses, our selfishness, and our failures in relationships and achievement. In effect, it comes when we set our lives beside the life of Christ. Herein is the genesis of the debate that Jim Collins appropriately triggered in his book *Good to Great*. It remains a difficult challenge for the Christian believer to publicly display such virtues, perceived as soft, in today's globally competitive, fast-paced culture. The Greeks had an adjective for humility which means "slavish." Since a word is known by the company it keeps, let's look at some other words used to describe humility from two different worldviews.

Leading Change Action Learning Lesson 4

Humility (Greek)	Humility (Judeo-Christian)
Slavish	Modeling Servanthood
Ignoble	Noble
Cowering	Courageous
Fearful	Confident
Servile	Service Oriented

Task 4.1 Interactive Action Learning

Great leaders are forever following and forever leading. That is, they are submitted to the rule of law, legal authorities, a board, a CEO or president, and so forth. What or whom are you submitted to in acting upon delegated authority, responsibility, and accountability?

Task 4.2 Interactive Action Learning

How would you characterize the leaders you are submitted to (e.g., caring or inconsiderate; humble or arrogant; open or closed)?	What do these qualities or actions evoke in you as a follower? List your corresponding action to their behavior.

Task 4.3 Interactive Action Learning

Given the best you can imagine, how would you most like to be seen by those within your sphere of influence? You might brainstorm ten or more qualities or behaviors, then list the five most important (as they help you lead those under your care or delegated responsibility).

Task 4.4 Interactive Action Learning

Given your list of the top five qualities or behaviors, what beliefs or actions do you most desire to evoke in those within your sphere of influence (e.g., mutual trust and respect, open and honest communication, a sense of freedom to grow and make decisions, a shared vision, quality workmanship, and so forth)? What is the best you can imagine and work toward as a more effective leader?

Team Building, Team Learning, and Teamwork

"When highly motivated, confident, goal-directed, and resourceful team players are 'carried beyond themselves,' your organization's competitive edge will widen considerably" (Bil Holton, in *Leading Change in Your World*, p. 81). Essentially, Holton is describing a collective intelligence, a creative synergy, and a generative learning team that results when individuals become part of a winning team, department, or unit within the company. John Maxwell says, "Teamwork makes the dreamwork." He champions the idea that building generative teams in an organization is the key to obtaining and maintaining the competitive edge in today's fast-paced global economy. We expand the notion that teamwork, creative work, smart work, and hard work make the dreamwork.

UNIT TWO
Leadership, Team Building, and Team Learning

WEEK 5
All Together Now! Collaborating with a Team

∼ **OBJECTIVE** ∼

The *Leading Change* learner will expand their understanding of team learning and assess how the process is being implemented in their unit or organization using the Team Performing Rating Form.

Assignments

1. Read Chapters 4 and 5 of the book *Leading Change in Your World*.

2. We expect that you have read through the entire book during the first few weeks. Now go back, studying and referencing the respective chapters for Week 4.

Leading Change Action Learning Lesson 5

Task 5.1 Interactive Action Learning

Following is a Team Performing Rating Form. How well are teams functioning in your organization? To what extent are effective team learning and team playing behaviors and practices being embedded in the culture of your organization? Take a few minutes to study the following self-assessment. Then thoughtfully and honestly complete the self-assessment. After photocopying this assessment, ask others within your sphere of influence to complete it, then reflect upon where you are in the process and consider how you and others might change.

What is Team Learning? Team building is not team learning. Team learning takes place when teams of coworkers engage in daily or routine conversation, inquiry, dialogue, collaboration, joint planning, and coordinated action to continuously improve people, systems, and processes leading to more good things and fewer bad things happening in the unit or organization. These team-learning actions enable the collective intelligence, intuition, and creativity of people engaged in a shared vision to energize one another to make extraordinary things happen.

Team Performing Rating Form: Think how your team would rate on a scale of 1-5. Directions: 1 = low; 5 = high. Underscore your response.

1 = Low to 5 = High

Mission, Core Values, and Vision

1.	Members can describe and are committed to a common mission.	1	2	3	4	5
2.	Goals are clear, challenging, and relevant to mission.	1	2	3	4	5
3.	Strategies for achieving goals are clear.	1	2	3	4	5
4.	Individual roles are clear; mission merges with position.	1	2	3	4	5

Empowerment and Equipping

5.	Members feel a personal and collective sense of power.	1	2	3	4	5
6.	Members have access to necessary skills and resources.	1	2	3	4	5
7.	Policies and practices support team objectives.	1	2	3	4	5
8.	Mutual respect and willingness to help each other is evident.	1	2	3	4	5

Relationships, Trust, and Communication

9.	Members express themselves openly and honestly.	1	2	3	4	5
10.	Warmth, understanding, and acceptance is expressed.	1	2	3	4	5
11.	Members listen actively and respectfully to each other.	1	2	3	4	5
12.	Differences of opinion and perspective are valued.	1	2	3	4	5

Creativity, Adaptability, and Flexibility

13.	Members perform different roles and functions as needed.	1	2	3	4	5
14.	Teams share responsibility for leadership and development.	1	2	3	4	5
15.	Members are adaptable to changing demands.	1	2	3	4	5
16.	Best alternative ideas, approaches, and solutions are explored.	1	2	3	4	5

Optimal Execution and Productivity

17.	Output is high.	1	2	3	4	5
18.	Quality is excellent.	1	2	3	4	5
19.	Decision making is informed, shared, and effective.	1	2	3	4	5
20.	Clear problem-solving process is apparent.	1	2	3	4	5

Recognition and Appreciation

21.	Individual contributions are recognized and appreciated by leader and other members; encouraging and complimenting.	1	2	3	4	5
22.	Team accomplishments are recognized by members.	1	2	3	4	5
23.	Team members feel trusted and respected.	1	2	3	4	5
24.	Team contributions are publicly valued and recognized.	1	2	3	4	5

Belonging and Morale

25.	Individuals feel good about their membership on the team.	1	2	3	4	5
26.	Individuals are competent, confident, and motivated.	1	2	3	4	5
27.	Teams have a sense of pride and satisfaction about their work.	1	2	3	4	5
28.	There is a strong sense of cohesion and team spirit.	1	2	3	4	5

Task 5.2 Interactive Action Learning

Given the Team Performing Rating Form, how do you feel about the team learning taking place in your unit or organization?

What five actions (see items 1-28) are you willing to take to increase the use of teams or improve their effectiveness within your organization? (Team building is not team learning. Team learning takes place when teams of coworkers engage in ongoing conversation, inquiry, dialogue, collaboration, joint planning, and coordinated action to continuously improve people, systems, and processes leading to more good things and fewer bad things happening in the unit or organization.)

How will the above list of five actions make things better in your unit or organization? What are the perceived and anticipated benefits?

Creating a Shared Vision and Strategic Plan

WEEK **6**

Bringing Order Out of Chaos: Conceptualizing the Vision

∞ OBJECTIVE ∞

The *Leading Change* learner will identify a compelling need—an urgent issue—that will serve as a vehicle through which the learner can act as a change facilitator in a life role.

Assignments

1. Read Chapters 5 and 6 of the book *Leading Change in Your World*.

2. We expect that you have read through the entire book during the first few weeks. Now, go back, studying and referencing the respective chapters for Week 6.

Leading Change Action Learning Lesson 6

"Never doubt that a small group of thoughtful, committed people can change the world; indeed it is the only thing that ever has" (p. 127). Note the focus is on a small group of thoughtful and committed people. There is no self-made millionaire. It took someone or an institution to provide the capital; someone to help create and deliver the service or product; someone to buy and use the product; and the list goes on. We are interdependent people. It takes a team of people to make more good things and fewer bad things happen.

Changing Your World. In previous lessons we have been looking at change from the inside out. We must experience change and understand change processes in order to be an agent of change in our sphere of influence. What is it that you would really like to change? Often it is something that you are sick and tired of; something that urgently needs to be changed; something that you are passionate about; something that will make this relationship or issue better for others and yourself. Let's look at an example of changes people have initiated.

Life Role – Sphere of Influence	Current Reality (What is)	Future Vision of Desired Result (What ought to be)
Parent	Lack of quality family time	Family growing, loving, and enjoying family activities more
Work	Low morale and inefficient systems	High morale, happy employees, efficient systems, and improved productivity – joy on the job
Church	Need more relevant adult Bible studies	Adult Bible school has tripled its size the first ninety days, and success stories are abounding
Community	Lack of wholesome recreational opportunities for teenagers in our town	Joint service organizations are opening up and equipping their facilities for more recreational opportunities for our youth

Compelling Need – Something that is Urgent to You and Others. Put on your red (passionate), green (creative), and yellow (optimistic) hats to identify something that you and those in your sphere of influence see and feel an urgent need to change. Spend some quality "thinking for a change" (John Maxwell) by completing the task below.

Task 6.1 Interactive Learning

Life Role – Sphere of Influence	Current Reality (What is)	Future Vision of Desired Result (What ought to be)
Example: Work	Our Project Team is overlooking too many small details in preparing bids and job quotes, resulting in missed deadlines and lost projects.	Project Team members are planning ahead, sharing quote and specification knowledge with one another, meeting all quote or bid deadlines, and celebrating the spirit of collaboration and teamwork.

Creating a Shared Vision and Strategic Plan

WEEK 7

Plotting the Course: Developing a Strategic Plan

∽ OBJECTIVE ∽

The *Leading Change* learner will build a "change team," inspire a shared vision, engage in analysis and decision making, and develop a strategic plan in response to a compelling need.

Assignments

1. Read Chapters 6 and 7 of the book *Leading Change in Your World*.

2. We expect that you have read through the entire book during the first few weeks. Now, go back, studying and referencing the respective chapters for Week 7.

An Eight-Step Change Process for Constructive Change

We have adapted Kotter's "Eight Steps for Successful Change" model (Kotter, John P. *Leading Change*. Boston: Harvard Business School Press, 1996.). The eight steps should be incorporated in a strategic planning design model and can also be used as criteria for implementing, monitoring, and assessing the change processes.

Step	Action	New Behavior
1	Identify a compelling need or increase a sense of urgency	People see and feel the need to change. They are ready and willing to join in the process.
2	Build the change facilitation team – Project Team	A team inspired enough to create constructive change is formed and begins to engage in team learning.
3	Create the right shared vision	The Change Facilitation Team seeks the best right answer for the issue and creates a shared vision.
4	Communicate for buy-in	Other people in the organization begin to see, feel, and buy in to the need for change.
5	Empower organization-wide action	More people feel able to act on the shared vision and support in the implementation.
6	Celebrate short-term gains – share success stories	Momentum builds as people work toward the vision and begin to share the success stories and results of constructive change.
7	Stay the course – patience and perseverance	People make changes in attitudes, practices, systems, and reward programs to ensure fulfillment of the vision.
8	Institutionalize the right changes	New and winning attitudes, practices, and systems are embedded in the new culture and structure emerging with the change.

Leading Change Action Learning Lesson 7

Task 7.1 Interactive Action Learning (Engage with others in developing this plan.)

Need, Urgent Issue, or Problem:	What problem do you and others believe and feel needs to be changed?
Change Team	Who are the two to five individuals that will engage in team learning with you to bring about this much-needed change?
Shared Vision	What is the best your Change Team can imagine if this change were fully successful over time? Visualize the attainment, feel it, and change!
SMART Goal	What SMART goal did your Change Team write to successfully implement this change and fulfill the vision?
Action Steps	What action steps will enable the successful attainment of this change goal? Implement, monitor, measure, and improve!
Obstacles	What obstacles must be overcome to successfully implement this change?

Operationalizing the Plan and Getting the Results

WEEK **8**

Making It Work: Getting Intended Results

∽ OBJECTIVE ∽

The *Leading Change* learner will collaborate with a Change Facilitation Team to implement, monitor, and measure the intended results of the unit or organizational change (i.e., shared vision and strategic plan).

Assignments

1. Read Chapters 7 and 8 of the book *Leading Change in Your World*.

2. We expect that you have read through the entire book during the first few weeks. Now, go back, studying and referencing the respective chapters for Week 8.

Making Change Strategies Work

In our combined years of leadership, we have watched companies and large organizations initiate change at the strategic planning level, but fail to implement the change successfully in the culture, structure, and systems of the organization. Too much time is spent in creating a strategic plan and too little time is spent engaging in operationalizing the vision, goals, and enabling actions. As Will Rogers says, *"Even if you're on the right track, you'll get run over if you just sit there"* (p. 149).

Reculturing. In the previous lesson we shared with you the eight-step change process adapted from Kotter. A study of this process reveals that this is both a reculturing and an implementation series of actions. Identifying a compelling need, creating a sense of urgency, galvanizing a change facilitation team, inspiring a shared vision of what could be, and beginning the process of planning, implementing, monitoring, and measuring the change results are critical to moving from "current reality to a desired state of future results." This is the process of team learning (i.e., conversations, inquiry, collaboration, reflection, team planning, and team actions). Team learning is the key to facilitating constructive change. It is a process of persistently and consistently implementing the plan and determining what is working and what can be done better. It is a process of "finding a better way every day" (Welch) that energizes people and produces results.

Operationalizing and Institutionalizing Constructive Change. You have worked with a Change Facilitation Team to develop a shared vision and strategic plan for initiating constructive change in a unit or organization. The action steps and obstacles or barriers along the way must be overcome. Patience (perseverance) is the key to successfully implementing and institutionalizing this change. Never give up. That is where many changes fail. You must be determined enough and passionate enough to never admit defeat or failure; to never give up until the vision is realized. Stay the course. The eight steps we have adapted from Kotter go a long way in building the change team and empowering unit-wide or organization-wide buy-in and commitment to something that is a compelling, urgent, and worthwhile cause. When you, your team, and others really see it and feel it, they will help to change it. Red hat feeling, thinking, and determination are critical to the process of fulfilling the vision.

Task 8.1 Interactive Action Learning

Eight Steps to Successfully Implement Constructive Change Assessment		
Step	**Action**	**Progress – How Well Are These Steps Being Implemented?**
1	Identify a compelling need or increase a sense of urgency	Good 1 2 3 4 5 Great
2	Build the change facilitation team – Project Team	Good 1 2 3 4 5 Great
3	Create the right shared vision	Good 1 2 3 4 5 Great
4	Communicate for buy-in	Good 1 2 3 4 5 Great
5	Empower organization-wide action	Good 1 2 3 4 5 Great
6	Celebrate short-term gains – share success stories	Good 1 2 3 4 5 Great
7	Stay the course – patience and perseverance	Good 1 2 3 4 5 Great
8	Institutionalize the right changes	Good 1 2 3 4 5 Great

Task 8.2 Interactive Action Learning

Given the eight-step assessment in task #1, what steps are being implemented well?

Which of the steps should now be implemented or can be implemented better?

How might you use these eight steps to assess previous unit or organizational change, or implement new changes in the future?

Anything worth doing is worth doing imperfectly
until you can do it perfectly —
the essence of continuous improvement.

UNIT FOUR
Operationalizing the Plan and Getting the Results

WEEK 9

Staying the Course: Overcoming Obstacles

∞ **OBJECTIVE** ∞

The *Leading Change* learner will now incorporate the Leading Change Assessment Model in preparing to assess or in assessing the unit or organizational change.

Assignments

1. Read Chapters 8 and 9 of the book *Leading Change in Your World*.

2. We expect that you have read through the entire book during the first few weeks. Now, go back, studying and referencing the respective chapters for Week 9.

Leading Change Action Learning Lesson 9

Results: The Challenge of Leadership is to Change Continuously
The challenge of twenty-first-century leadership is to lead the necessary change that is continuously finding a better way—being open to new possibilities. "The challenge of leadership on any level—individual, family, workplace, church, or community—is to change continuously while remaining unified in promoting the common good" (Lindsay).

Assessment Model. Figure 7.1 (p. 159) shows a six-step Assessment Model. The authors have frequently found that for individuals, units, and organizations, change often disintegrates during the implementation process. This process demands a balance between advocacy and inquiry; control and flexibility; creativity and accountability; vision and values. It requires a process of delegated authority, project team responsibility, and accountability. When assessment and accountability are vague or undefined, the intended change loses vision and value to the internal and external benefactors. Therefore, the assessment model ensures the proper authority, responsibility, and accountability to produce the envisioned results.

Task 9.1 Interactive Action Learning

Assess the Intended Results: Think Through the Assessment Model	
Assessment Steps	**Assessment Thinking and Planning**
1. Select a goal.	State the SMART Goal written in lesson #7.
2. Select an assessment measure.	What is the best measure that your change facilitation team could use to assess the progress and results of this change?
3. List performance criteria.	What performance indicators will demonstrate successful attainment of the goal for this change?
4. Collect and analyze data.	What quarterly performance data will we collect for analysis and decision making (see PISCO, chapter 6, p. 133).
5. Compare new data to existing data.	What were the unsatisfactory facts, numbers, and indicators that prompted the need to change? How is the change affecting those data?
6. Recommend changes.	What quarterly feedback data indicate a need to make course corrections in the strategic plan for change? What adjustments need to be made in implementing the new change (see Kotter's eight steps)?

"The more a project team is empowered to solve its problems through constructive change, the healthier it is."

Larry Lindsay

Operationalizing the Plan and Getting the Results

WEEK 10

Get Up and Get Going: Being an Agent of Change

∾ OBJECTIVE ∾

The *Leading Change* learner will reflect upon the rich life-learning experiences of this course and summarize the value-added benefits to them and to those within their sphere of influence.

Assignments

1. Read Chapters 9 and 10 of the book *Leading Change in Your World*.

2. We expect that you have read through the entire book during the first few weeks. Now, go back, studying and referencing the respective chapters for Week 10.

Leading Change Action Learning Lesson 10

Leaders as Learner: Being the Lead Learner

When we are learning, we are changing – growing – maturing – improving – becoming – living. Approximately 80 percent of adult learning comes from reflecting upon rich life experience. As we make meaning in rich life experiences, we find new things to learn, new skills to develop, best practices to master and implement, and ways to influence the improvement of people and units or organizations in our sphere of influence.

Task 10.1 Interactive Action Learning

If experience (i.e., doing, reflecting, and changing—getting better) is the best teacher, what have you learned during the "Leading Change In Your World" adult learning, self-directed course?

Task 10.2 Interactive Action Learning

In what ways has this self-directed learning experience added value to who you are and your ability to add value to people and units or organizations?

Task 10.3 Interactive Action Learning

How strongly are you committed to achieving your two SMART goals and action plans?

What progress have you made in implementing these two SMART goals and action plans?

"It's not where you start but how you finish that counts."

Zig Ziglar

Endnotes

1. Fullan, M. (2002). *Leading in a Culture of Change*. San Francisco: Jossey Bass Publications.

2. Smith, M. & Lindsay, L. *(2004). Leading Change in Your World. Marion, IN: Triangle Publishing*.

3. Lindsay, L. (2003). *Mega Leadership*. (Submitted for publication: *Strategies for Today's Leaders*.)